Captured Moments

In Time

Christine V. Bell LCSW

BookLeaf Publishing
India | USA | UK

Made with ❤ on the BookLeaf Publishing Platform
www.bookleafpub.in
www.bookleafpub.com

Dedication

For those who read between the lines.

Preface

This book of was not written in order.
It was written in moments.
Some of the pieces are exact memories.
Some are condensed reflections.
Some are conversations I had with myself
that I decided not to keep private.
They are not explanations.
They are not instructions.
They are not conclusions.
They are captured moments in time.
What they mean to you
may change with time.
What they mean to me
already has.
Read slowly.
Read honestly.
And if something feels familiar,
sit with it.

Acknowledgements

This book is not a conclusion.
It is a record
of what I noticed
while becoming.

1. Still

Stillness at times
when silence sets in
and the blurry
becomes sharply clear
I see the motions
that got me
to this place.

2. What Was Left

You cannot make a person
want better for themselves,
no matter how hard you try.

They have to want it
for themselves.

And that leaves a bitter taste
in your mouth
when you were their caretaker
and they became a part of you.

So you try
and try.

But despite the energy
and effort,
they leave you
holding a bag
they never filled.

And you are left
gathering the pieces
you never broke.

3. Before Falling

Why I never fell in love
Funny question.
The truth is,
I was never picked up enough
to fall.
If falling in love were a choice,
you would first have to be
given the option.
Right?
I learned early
love is expensive,
and the price became too high
when it required me.
When you are told
you are nothing,
trying to believe
you are worth anything
becomes its own journey.
So yes,
I never fell in love.

I was never given
the option to fall.
But I was pushed
into finding
distorted definitions of love.
But fall?
No.
I haven't
fallen in love.

4. A Thought About God

One of my Constance thoughts
is whether God hears me.
Not prayers for things,
or people,
or even myself.
I mean my tears.
I was thinking back
to a time in childhood,
now that my system feels safe enough
to remember.
I remember standing high above the world,
crying,
wondering if my absence
would matter.
Pain has a way
of wanting instant relief,
even in childhood.
I remember the weight of the moment,
not because of fear,
but because the pain shifted.

I thought
who would care for my mother
if I were not here?
I must have been
six or seven.
Thinking about it now,
I can see how it was buried,
blocked out.
But now
it reminds me
how early we learn
to choose our cages.

5. The Other Side

The villain is the bad guy to me
the villain is person who stood up for themselves
and wasn't socially approved of.
Villains aren't self made.
No one is born bad.
Life gives you a set of cards
and you play them.
You work with what you have,
and that is considered bad
when it isn't socially acceptable.
Well, fuck the hero
who chose to deny themselves
every part of life
just to be acceptable.
Who created these norms?
What is socially acceptable
when being social
is not always acceptable?
So I root for the villain sometimes,
until a mirror is held

to society's face.
Change can never happen
or even be discussed
if no one confronts it first.
No one heals
what they do not confront.
So hats off
to the misfits,
the black sheep,
the unacceptable ones.

6. Unseen

It took me sometime
to see myself as beautiful.
Growing up,
hearing my skin was too dark
didn't help much.
I didn't like myself
or any parts of me.
Funny how
I could see more flaws
than beauty.
So I compared myself to no one
you have to have self-worth
to do that.
I hid behind clothing at times.
Come to think of it,
I didn't have to hide much.
I was already invisible anyway.
I spent the better part of my life
not believing in me,

valuing myself as less.
I remember when that all changed
with the help of a person
I am no longer connected to.
However,
she was one person
I felt connected to
or at least I thought.
Truthfully,
I hadn't found her.
I had found me.
I found my voice,
my purpose,
and my definition of beauty.
I discovered what was within,
and nothing outside
has measured up
since.

7. How I Listen

Music
the way it flows through your body
and matches your mood effortlessly.
The way one song can touch you,
or make you recall memories
of good times
or not so good ones.
As long as I can remember,
music was my primary language.
I used it to communicate my emotions
the way a writer uses words
or God uses people.
I have a song for every mood.
Music carries memories
of the past,
the present,
and parts of my future.
I know no matter what's going on,
there is a song for that
a melody to match.

I know some artist is killing me softly,
or reminding me
that I shall overcome.
Music is the forever mood.
The way a painter uses a brush,
I use music
and it uses me.

8. One Life

I had my heartbroken
in a dream once.
I remember going to sleep,
and the last question I asked was
why didn't me and someone
with mutual attraction
work out?
We were good together.
We had the same values.
She off.
I didn't care.
We all have a type.
So I made that statement
before I went to sleep,
and had what felt like
the longest dream.
We were married.
It had to be the 1970s.
A beautiful family.
I could feel

how deeply I loved her,
and how beautiful she was
even in my dream.
I recall the dream now
as a memory
rather than a dream,
because it feels that way.
I remember fast-forwarding
into the future.
I was caring for our children
and was with another woman.
As she walked down the hall,
I could feel her energy.
She was still beautiful,
even though I was not with her.
I remember telling my daughter,
"Mommy's coming."
Someone asked,
why did y'all break up?
My memory went
to her birthday.
I was hiding a gift
under the bed.
She walked in.
I smiled.
It felt different.
I asked her to follow me

down the steps
to a lower apartment.
She did
smiling,
holding my hand.
I opened the door,
moved a divider,
and there sat a man
with three children.
She jumped back,
shocked.
I stood there
as one of the children yelled,
"Mommy."
She looked up from the chair
with tears.
She said nothing.
I said,
"This is what you were doing
while you were visiting your mother."
She said,
"I can explain."
He sat there,
said nothing.
The children called to her.
I remember asking them to leave.
We would talk later.

I told him and the children
they were family
and would be provided for accordingly.
She ran upstairs.
I followed
hurt,
yelling.
I asked the children
to go into their rooms.
We closed our door.
I remember the hurt
deep hurt.
I was broken.
I remember her
trying to fix it.
I remember being sexual
and wanting her
while broken,
which broke me more.
I woke up.
And those love songs
hit different that day.

9. After the Fire

Feelings are not facts.
That's easy to say
when the facts
are not what you want them to be.

But my feelings
are a matter of my facts.

They are my internal
written work.

They shouldn't be dismissed,
because they are indeed facts.

They are based on me
and all that makes up me.

My feelings matter,
therefore they are
a matter of fact.

So what if they change
and are sometimes
all over the place?

They are floating facts.
They make up
all that is me.

And I matter.
Right?

I mean
if my feelings aren't facts,
then why do they feel
so factual to me?

Why does hurt
feel tight,
and happiness
feel light?

Those are facts, right?

So why,
when you are uncomfortable,
are they not facts?

They may not be your facts,
but they are my facts.

And that matters.

10. Just Being

Who am I?
Shit, I don't know
you tell me.
There is a category
for everything
and everyone.
I just label myself as me,
whoever the fuck that is today.
I may be a writer,
a counselor,
an artist,
or an activist.
I wear many, many hats.
And today
just for today
I would like
to just be.
That is a thing, right?
To just be?
Just here,

in the skin that I am,
enjoying the simple things in life.
No titles.
No labels.
No one depending on me,
asking me,
wanting me,
or needing me
for a damn thing.
Can I be like the air
and just provide,
but not be seen?
Can there be
no expectations
attached to me?
Can everything
just fade,
and I just be
right now?
A whisper,
something said
and only heard
by a few.
Who am I?
Can I be words
and be used properly
and accounted for?

Can I be silence
and carry the weight of the world
without a name?
Can I be music
and touch
without hands?
Can I be safety
and provide comfort?
Can I just be
today?

11. A Long Time Ago

I met you
by accident
on purpose.

I didn't even know
if we spoke
the same language.

And we did.
We enjoyed
the same things
and shared
some of the same past.

I remember the days
we were together.

I wanted it
to last forever.

And it did
until forever
added a day.

12. What I Feel

Have you ever experienced
a slow burn in real life
not in love,
but in loss?

The moment
that plays over
and over again,
until it plays out
like a match.

It starts off strong,
and when it ends,
all you have
is slight smoke
and the smell
of something
that was.

Is that what grief feels like

a slow burn
that never goes out,
but over time
becomes more manageable,
more measurable?

13. Than and Now

I don't miss you.
I miss who I was with you.

I was trusting,
romantic,
and open.

I miss that side of myself.

I miss how sweet I was
late-night calls and texts.
I couldn't go a day
without expressing something,
in some way.

I was new
and innocent.

I miss that part of me
that could trust

without question,
and believe in
love at first sight.

I miss that part of me
that had no questions.

And don't get me wrong
I love this version of me.

But that version
had something
this version didn't.

Belief.

That what you give,
you get.

She gave freely
when she should have
charged interest.
She should have had
no interest
and instead invested in herself.

She gave a lot

and expected so little.
That one right there
she was naïve.

But even naïve
has its place.
Even naïve
has its protection.
Even naïve
allows you some grace.

This version right here
this version is not naïve.
She can see clearly.
So when she makes decisions,
she makes them
knowing the consequences
of her actions.
She weighs them clearly.
She grasps everything
she wouldn't have
when she was that version
of herself.

That version couldn't see,
because she thought
everyone believed

the way she believed.
She thought the heart
would never be
taken for granted.
So she granted access.
Then she granted leaves and excused the abstance.

And when they returned,
they gave no thanks.
So she granted permission
to full disrespect.

That girl
I do miss her, though.
Some days
I see her
looking back at me.
I dismiss her.
She has no place
here.

14. For the Girls

I turned nothing
into something.
They didn't believe.
Told me I'd fail.
Shit
I didn't believe in myself either.
Truthfully,
I stopped thinking of myself
and started thinking,
I hope heaven is nice,
because I'm living in hell.
Degrees don't help that.
A hood birth.
Living in shelters.
Taught her to tote that.
I don't know what's worse
the streets
or living with family.
Both carry the same hurt.
At least outside,

you can hide
what's inside.
I didn't take my first sip
until I was eighteen.
After that,
I won't lie
it felt addictive.
It healed quick.
Wake up.
Go to school.
Back to the same shit
pain and pressure,
from the same girl.
Hiding my sexuality
felt like a living bid.
Wait
no hood talk.
Let me use proper words.
I was in a tunnel,
and the dark
was the only light I knew.
No one asked
if I was okay.
As long as I showed up
and performed.
Paid my own way.
My momma told me

money was the only reason
family allowed us
in their home.
Damn.
That brought me back
to that space.
I remember watching
my grandmother die.
Oh wait
they held that part.
They left us.
Family ain't shit.
I know that part.
Wait.
Hold on.
I practice forgiveness.
But what happens
when forgiveness
forgets to include
accountability?
But we don't talk about that.
I'm writing these words
directly from the heart.
No tears.
No anger.
Just feelings
and facts.

Wait
damn.

(Breath)

Feelings aren't facts.

15. As It Is

To my five young Black Queens
I pray that each of you
be all that you want to be.
As young Black women,
always remember
you are queens,
and nobody on this earth
can hold you back
or tone you down.
You are the definition of love.
From the first day I met you,
you took a piece of my heart.
I knew you would be great.
And you already are
so smart,
funny,
and kind.
I adore that about you.
Seeing you grow
is a blessing.

I hope you become
everything you aim for.
The sky will never be your limit.
Follow your own voice.
Know you are always loved,
no matter where you go.
Your heart is protected.
Praise be to God first.
May angels always surround
and watch over you.
Although you are not mine by birth,
the blessing of being your godmother
is a title I wear proudly.
There is nothing like it.
I get to spoil you
without diapers.
Love and blessings
to each of your parents.
No matter what happened
in their relationship,
they made you
and I am blessed for that.
They will forever
have my respect.
I want you to know
you were always wanted,
always prayed for.

On days you may feel unwanted,
remember that.
Stand tall.
You are the table,
not the floor.
God will always prepare
a table before you,
so don't worry about enemies.
He leads you
and guides you
through any valley
you may cross.

16. Grateful

Grateful.

17. Anchor

My Mom is my anchor.
And as I write this,
I realize she keeps me still
while underwater.
She holds a place for me
while her mind works against her daily
something she can't help.
When she was becoming,
there was no room for growth.
She had to be
when she wasn't ready.
Her mind did what minds do best
it protected her
at the cost of her.
I watched my mother
lose touch with reality
while ensuring
I held onto mine.
She was the cause
of my trauma

and works daily
to help me work through it.
Like an anchor does.
She stands tied.
Change changes.
People change.
Places change.
And she holds still.
I am amazed by her,
yet curious.
Because when reality is often tested,
what is true and what is not
holds a different meaning
to the child
who witnessed it all.
I have heard
some of the wisest words
come from her.
And when unstable,
some of the most brutal.
I guess an anchor
comes with both
the good
and the bad.
She instilled in me
faith and worship,
respect and kindness,

accountability and truth.
Gifts she learned
on her own.
I am convinced
God's greatest blessing
is her fried chicken
and smart remarks.
I love her energy,
although it comes with a cost.
What stabilizes me
also holds me still.
Anchors can become heavy
at times.
And the want
no, the need
to detach
becomes attractive.
Then I remember
I am as much hers
as she is mine.
Because of that,
I understand
comfort isn't always comfortable,
and love
has different forms
and shapes.
While I will never agree

that pain is love,
I understand
what a mother endures
comes from a place of love.
And for that,
I am grateful
daily.
So I enjoy my anchor
daily,
as it has more days behind it
than in front of it.
One day,
that stability will be gone,
and what was learned
will become
the new anchor.
So I take notes
as often
as possible.

18. Distance

I developed fa case of friendship numbness
after enduring
one toxic friendship
after another.
My symptoms are
clear communication,
boundaries,
and emotional regulation.
I am always prepared
to lose a friend,
even if the bond is tight.
I learned from
the countless friendships
I lost
due to being honest,
standing on my word,
and truthfulness.
I would have survived
if I had just learned
to forget

and accept the disrespect
something I could not do.
I had another that came after,
and I thought this one
was going to be the one.
We had so much trauma in common
that we bonded quickly.
Plus, blood
made us tighter.
I thought this one
would survive.
But again,
I was required
to excuse catfish lies
and manipulation.
I had another
when I was younger
that I remember so clearly.
I had two good friends.
I made one,
then another.
Then both disappeared.
It came to find out
one lied between the two of us,
and the three of us
quietly faded away.
As she stood in the middle

and laughed about the deceit,
I learned the manipulation
had been going on
since day one.
And I swear
I have friendship numbness.
The symptoms vary.
I've tried several cures
being alone,
being isolated.
But it tends not to work.
They say as you heal,
you attract more
of what's like you.
But even when you do,
the memories of the past
still plague me.
I swear
I have friendship numbness.
So now I'm really clear.
I tend to medicate myself
by being honest.
But truthfully,
I have friendship numbness.
So I don't call people
best friends.
That title is retired.

What was best to me
wasn't best to them.
If you asked them now,
I'd probably be the liar.
I tend to look at things
from both sides.
Maybe showing up,
being there,
and holding them down
was the wrong thing to do.
They say God teaches lessons.
Maybe I shouldn't have
showed up
for that interview.
I have
friendship numbness.

19. Finding My Sound

honestly didn't know
what I sounded like.
I knew I had a voice.
I knew I had an internal voice.
I had a perception
of what I sounded like,
but I had no idea
what I actually sounded like.
Wait.
I had no idea
what I sounded like.
At one point,
I thought I sounded
like a waste of time.
At another point,
I thought I sounded
like a career.
I thought I sounded
like a lawyer.
I thought I sounded

like an activist.
I thought I sounded
like a volunteer.
I thought I sounded
like a politician.
At one point,
I even thought
I sounded like a mother.
At another point,
I knew I sounded confused.
At another point,
I thought I sounded
like a friend.
At one point,
I thought I was too loud.
Then another,
I thought I was too quiet.
The internal voice
changed with the external voice.
And I got to a point
where I thought
I knew what I sounded like.
I once thought
I knew what I sounded like
until I heard my voice.
And I realized
it sounded like wisdom.

It sounded like trust in oneself.
It sounded like pain.
It sounded like pleasure.
It sounded like love.
It sounded like hate sometimes.
It sounded like confusion.
It sounded like wanting.
It sounded like coming in.
Sometimes it sounded like going.
My voice began to take on
all these different sounds.
I swear,
I would have thought
I had multiple personalities,
but in order for that to be true,
I wouldn't know
the others existed.
So I had to realize
the sound I was making
was just me
becoming.
And I didn't know
what I was becoming.
At one point,
I thought I wanted
to be a doctor.
I thought I wanted to be

I thought I wanted to be
I didn't know
what I wanted to be.
Knowing what I wanted to be
came when I thought
I was what I was supposed to be.
Then I remembered
I wasn't even supposed
to be here.
So I paused.
I didn't want to hear
my own voice anymore.
When I heard
what I sounded like,
it scared me.
When people began
to pay attention,
I became frightened.
Do they hear
the same sound I hear?
Do they hear
the imperfections?
I know people worry
about seeing imperfections,
but it's another thing
to hear them.
Because if I look perfect

but don't sound perfect,
does that make me perfect?
So I became quiet again
because I didn't know
what I sounded like.
Wait.
I know exactly
what I sounded like.
I used to sound like strength.
Then I had moments
that weakened me.
I laid in bed,
crying,
and said to myself,
"If this is what strength sounds like,
then I have to find strength
with no tears."
And I didn't know
what my tears sounded like.
So I was still wondering,
what did I sound like?
But at least now
I was wondering.
Then I hurt myself again,
and I asked,
why do I still wonder
what I sound like

when I'm supposed
to have one voice?
If my sound is supposed to change,
am I going through puberty?
Does my voice crack
and break?
I know my back cracks
and breaks,
and it hurts.
But I'm told to get up.
I'm a strong Black woman—
get up.
You know what you sound like.
You sound like your ancestors.
You sound like your past.
You sound like those
who wore whips
on their backs.
You sound like change.
You sound like the Middle Passage.
So is that what I sound like?
Do I sound like
those who came before me?
Is that what I'm supposed
to sound like?
And I became unsure again.
Then I lost my sound.

Then life began to happen,
and it became so noisy
that I couldn't find my sound.
Then life began to slow down.
And I began to hear
my own voice.
And now,
I recognize
what I sound like.
And I don't sound like
any of those things.
I have remorse
because how can I not sound like
what I came from?
Shouldn't I sound like
where I've been?

20. In Time

The assignment was to write a letter to myself.
I never know what to say to myself.
There are too many parts of me.
Trauma made me.
Poverty raised me.
Ancestors bathed me,
and the world discriminated against me.
Food insecurities taught me how to walk.
Being Black and spiritual taught me how to talk.
I learned to love from the Bible
and how to hate from its rival.
I learned how to do math
hanging around MLK Ave
the same place where I learned chemistry.
Biology was taught to me
through violations of my body,
and reading was taught to me
by Reading Rainbow, thanks to PBS Channel 13.
I learned art through graffiti,
and gym was regularly taught

by local police.
I learned cooking by the stove
and measurements by neighbor tutors.
I never know what to say to me
because I never know
which part of me I'm talking to.
Truthfully,
am I talking to the hope
or the faith?
Am I supposed to talk to the Black girl lost
or the woman she became?
Am I addressing the letter,
"Dear young one,"
or "Hi from beyond the man-made grave"?
Yeah,
I don't know what to put down on this page.
I'll save it
for another day.

21. Love

I stood still.
What was left before falling
was a thought about God
and the other side.
Because I felt unseen,
I had to learn how to listen to myself,
reminding myself daily
that I only have one life.
And after the fires of that life
that once consumed me,
I began to understand
how just being
is a gift.
A long time ago,
during a still moment,
I reflected on my life,
and what I felt then
and what I feel now
for the girl I once was
as it is today

is gratitude.
Gratitude for all of these moments
that anchor me
and distance me,
so that I could find my sound.
And in time,
I found it.
And it sounds,
and feels,
like love.

www.ingramcontent.com/pod-product-compliance
Lightning Source LLC
Chambersburg PA
CBHW070646240926
51846CB00003BA/799
9789375270027